KINGFISHER

First published 2007 by Kingfisher
This edition published 2011 by Kingfisher
an imprint of Macmillan Children's Books
a division of Macmillan Publishers Limited
20 New Wharf Road, London N1 9RR
Basingstoke and Oxford
Associated companies throughout the world
www.panmacmillan.com

ISBN 978-0-7534-3389-8

Science consultant: Dr Christopher Hutchinson
Consultant: Dr Mark Winter
Dr Winter is a senior lecturer in chemistry at the University of Sheffield and the author of
www.webelements.com. This book uses data adapted from www.webelements.com.
Designed and created by Basher www.basherbooks.com
Dedicated to Ella Marbrook

9 8 7 6 5 4 3 2 1
1TR/0911/SC/WKT/140MA

A CIP catalogue record for this book is available from the British Library.

Printed in China

Note to readers: the website address listed above is correct at the time of going to print. However,
due to the ever-changing nature of the internet, website addresses and content can change.
Websites can contain links that are unsuitable for children. The publisher cannot be held
responsible for changes in website addresses or content, or for information obtained through
a third party. We strongly advise that internet searches should be supervised by an adult.

CONTENTS

The Periodic Table

Introduction

Everything in the world is made of elements – substances that cannot be broken down or made into anything simpler by chemical reactions. Each element has its own unique personality. Many, such as Gold, Silver and Lead, have been known for millennia. Others, such as Darmstadtium, have been created in high-tech labs, only as recently as the 1990s.

The periodic table was the brainchild of Siberian super-chemist, Dimitri Mendeleev. In 1869, he arranged the known elements into groups (columns) and periods (rows), leaving gaps in his table for chemical elements still undiscovered at the time. These days the gaps have been filled and there are a total of 111 known elements, but there may be others yet undiscovered. The vertical groups of the table make up "families" – all closely related and liking the same sorts of chemical shenanigans. In this book you'll meet the most representative characters from each group, as well as the tearaways and mavericks who do things their own way…

Mendelevium (named after Mendeleev)

1 **Hydrogen**

* Symbol: H
* Atomic number: 1
* Atomic weight: 1.0079

* Colour: None
* Standard state: Gas at 25 °C
* Classification: Non-metallic

I may be undersized, but don't underestimate me. I'm a petite package who packs a punch and a fiery character to boot – always remember I'm *numero uno*! I am the simplest and lightest of all the elements, the most abundant in the Universe and the source of everything in it, from matter and energy to life. I'm what powers nuclear fusion in the stars and I'm the building block for all of the other elements of the periodic table.

On Earth, I exist as a gas consisting of a pair of hydrogen atoms (H_2). Things always go with a bang when I'm around. I'm extraordinarily flammable. I was once used to fill airships, until a few fatal explosions ended my career. In the future, I am set to become important in fuel cells – a clean and efficient way of generating electricity.

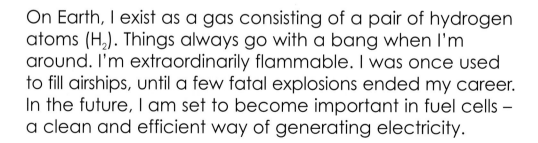

Date of discovery: 1766

* Density   0.082 g/l
* Melting point   −259.14 °C
* Boiling point   −252.87 °C

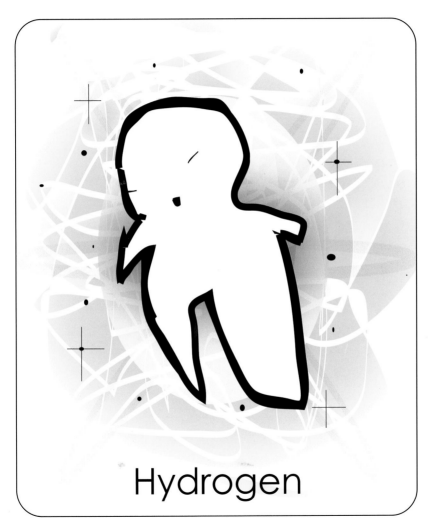

Hydrogen

CHAPTER 1

The Alkali Metals

A rowdy bunch of rebels, these elements have a reputation for extremely reactive behaviour. Chemically too feisty to be found unchanged in nature, this group are closer and more alike than any other group of the periodic table. All of them are low-density, soft metals. When added to water, they turn it alkaline. Their dangerous desperation to lose their outer electron increases with their atomic number, and as soon as they come into contact with almost anything (including the air), a violently explosive reaction follows...

THE PERIODIC

ONE WEEK LOAN

THE PERIODIC TABLE

1		
 H **HYDROGEN**		

3  Li **LITHIUM**	4 Be **BERYLLIUM**
11 Na **SODIUM**	12 Mg **MAGNESIUM**
19 K **POTASSIUM**	20 Ca **CALCIUM**
37 Rb **RUBIDIUM**	38 Sr **STRONTIUM**
55 Cs **CAESIUM**	56 Ba **BARIUM**
87 Fr **FRANCIUM**	88 Ra **RADIUM**

21 Sc SCANDIUM	22 Ti TITANIUM	23 V VANADIUM	24 Cr CHROMIUM	25 Mn MANGANESE	26 Fe IRON	27 Co COBALT	28 Ni NICKEL	29 Cu COPPER
39 Y YTTRIUM	40 Zr ZIRCONIUM	41 Nb NIOBIUM	42 Mo MOLYBDENUM	43 Tc TECHNETIUM	44 Ru RUTHENIUM	45 Rh RHODIUM	46 Pd PALLADIUM	47 Ag SILVER
57 La LANTHANUM	72 Hf HAFNIUM	73 Ta TANTALUM	74 W TUNGSTEN	75 Re RHENIUM	76 Os OSMIUM	77 Ir IRIDIUM	78 Pt PLATINUM	79 Au GOLD
89 Ac ACTINIUM	104 Rf RUTHERFORDIUM	105 Db DUBNIUM	106 Sg SEABORGIUM	107 Bh BOHRIUM	108 Hs HASSIUM	109 Mt MEITNERIUM	110 Ds DARMSTADTIUM	111 Rg ROENTGENIUM

58 Ce CERIUM	59 Pr PRASEODYMIUM	60 Nd NEODYMIUM	61 Pm PROMETHIUM	62 Sm SAMARIUM	63 Eu EUROPIUM	64 Gd GADOLINIUM	65 Tb TERBIUM	66 Dy DYSPROSIUM
90 Th THORIUM	91 Pa PROTACTINIUM	92 U URANIUM	93 Np NEPTUNIUM	94 Pu PLUTONIUM	95 Am AMERICIUM	96 Cm CURIUM	97 Bk BERKELIUM	98 Cf CALIFORNIUM

3

Li

LITHIUM

11

Na

SODIUM

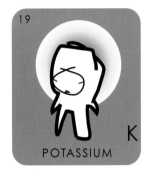

19

K

POTASSIUM

37

Rb

RUBIDIUM

55

Cs

CAESIUM

87

Fr

FRANCIUM

3 Lithium

■ The Alkali Metals

- ✹ Symbol: Li
- ✹ Atomic number: 3
- ✹ Atomic weight: 6.941

- ✹ Colour: Silvery grey/white
- ✹ Standard state: Solid at 25 °C
- ✹ Classification: Metallic

The lightest of all metals on the periodic table and the first, I am a real soft touch. You can easily slice me with a knife, but when I'm combined with other metals like Aluminium, I make really strong (and light) alloys. These qualities make me popular with the aerospace industry.

I am generally a useful and very helpful fellow. You can find me acting as the positive half of many batteries and as part of high-performance, industrial lubricants.

As lithium chloride (me plus Chlorine), I'm remarkably good at absorbing large amounts of water. Taken as lithium carbonate (me, Oxygen and Carbon), I help restore damaged personalities – calming and relieving sufferers of mental illnesses such as manic depression.

Date of discovery: 1817

- ● Density   0.535 g/cm³
- ● Melting point   180.54 °C
- ● Boiling point   1342 °C

Lithium

11 Sodium

■ The Alkali Metals

- ✷ Symbol: Na
- ✷ Atomic number: 11
- ✷ Atomic weight: 22.99
- ✷ Colour: Grey/white
- ✷ Standard state: Solid at 25 °C
- ✷ Classification: Metallic

I'm a complete livewire – highly strung and volatile – but I get along well with everyone and make strong, long-lasting friendships. I'm a grey-coloured metal that's soft enough to be cut with a knife. I'm really reactive – you need to store me under oil to stop me chemically reacting with the oxygen in the air, and I'll explode into flames on contact with water!

I form loads of common compounds like sodium chloride (salt) and sodium carbonate (dishwashing detergent) that are all solid and very stable due to their strong bonds. My ions (negative particles) are very soluble and are the reason why the sea is salty. I give street lights their orange glow, and I am used in nuclear reactors as a coolant, because I conduct heat really well.

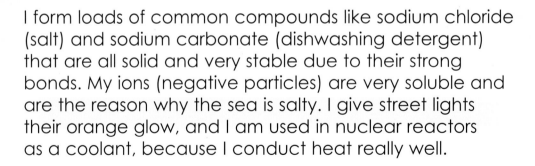

Date of discovery: 1807

- ● Density   0.968 g/cm³
- ● Melting point   97.72 °C
- ● Boiling point   883 °C

Sodium

19 **Potassium**

■ The Alkali Metals

- ❋ Symbol: K
- ❋ Atomic number: 19
- ❋ Atomic weight: 39.098

- ❋ Colour: Silver
- ❋ Standard state: Solid at 25 °C
- ❋ Classification: Metallic

I am Sodium's twin brother. I am soft and react with air, so storing me under oil is essential. This little precaution keeps me isolated from contact with air or water. My ions can be easily detected in any substance since they give off a bright lilac flame. Just as stunning is my explosive reaction with water, which is even stronger than that of my sibling Sodium.

Everyone knows I can be found in bananas, but I bet you didn't know that I am key to many processes in your body. Most vitally I aid the function of nerves, allowing the brain to transmit information to the muscles. But too much of me in the body can lead to a heart attack and this is my darker side – in the USA, potassium chloride is used in the lethal injections that kill Death Row prisoners.

Date of discovery: 1807

- ● Density   0.856 g/cm^3
- ● Melting point   63.38 °C
- ● Boiling point   759 °C

Potassium

37 **Rubidium**

■ The Alkali Metals

✳ Symbol: Rb
✳ Atomic number: 37
✳ Atomic weight: 85.468

✳ Colour: Silvery
✳ Standard state: Solid at 25 °C
✳ Classification: Metallic

I'm scarce and hard to find. If you do unearth me, you'll see that I am a master of disguise and can mimic my cousins in Group I. Like the rest of the gang, I'm super-reactive. I go off with a bang on contact with air or water. Since I'm so tricksy and rare, I'm very expensive. Watch out for me in the medicines of the future...

Rubidium

Date of discovery: 1861

Rb

● Density — 1.532 g/cm³
● Melting point — 39.31 °C
● Boiling point — 688 °C

Caesium 55
The Alkali Metals ■

* Symbol: Cs
* Atomic number: 55
* Atomic weight: 132.91

* Colour: Golden tinge
* Standard state: Solid at 25 °C
* Classification: Metallic

Caesium

Soft and golden, I'm way more exciting than Gold. When provoked I give off sky-blue light. Of my Group I gang, I have the fiercest reaction to water. I keep the beat in atomic clocks accurate to one second every several hundred thousand years! My nasty radioactive isotope, Caesium-137, was a major pollutant after the 1986 Chernobyl nuclear disaster.

Date of discovery: 1860

● Density   1.879 g/cm³
● Melting point 28.44 °C
● Boiling point 671 °C

 Cs

CHAPTER 2

The Alkaline Earth Metals

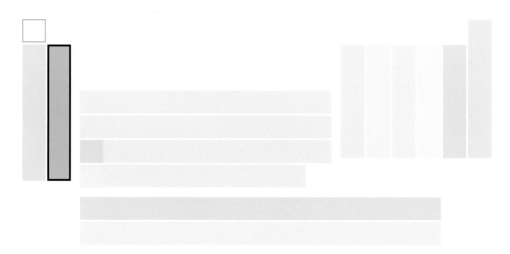

The "alkaline earths" were once thought to be totally harmless and boring, because they were always found tightly bonded to Oxygen. However, once released from these stable compounds, they began to act in the same unruly fashion as their next-door neighbours, the Group I family. Another gang of soft metals, these guys react easily and burn fiercely, getting meaner towards the base of the group. All are eager to lose their outer electrons, but this happens less easily than it does for the alkali metals, so they are a little less reactive.

4  **Be**	12  **Mg**	20 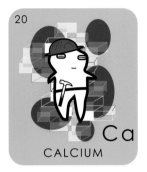 **Ca**
BERYLLIUM	MAGNESIUM	CALCIUM
38  **Sr**	56  **Ba**	88  **Ra**
STRONTIUM	BARIUM	RADIUM

4 Beryllium

■ The Alkaline Earth Metals

- ✳ Symbol: Be
- ✳ Atomic number: 4
- ✳ Atomic weight: 9.0122
- ✳ Colour: Silvery
- ✳ Standard state: Solid at 25 °C
- ✳ Classification: Metallic

Lucky for you, I am a shy and secretive chap and don't get out much. A small amount of me in your body can give you berylliosis, a disease that inflames the lungs and is linked to lung cancer. As a metal I am soft and silvery and I'm used mainly in metal alloys, in league with other metals. I make excellent electrical conductors and I'm very flexible too. Because I am so super-light I also get used in the manufacture of aeroplanes.

I'm often dug out of the ground as silicates – compounds I form with Silicon and other elements – the most beautiful of which is an emerald. My proudest moment came in 1932 when James Chadwick bombarded me with alpha particles and discovered the neutron. The neutrons I produce now play a leading role in nuclear chemistry.

Date of discovery: 1797

- ● Density   1.848 g/cm³
- ● Melting point   1287 °C
- ● Boiling point   2469 °C

Be

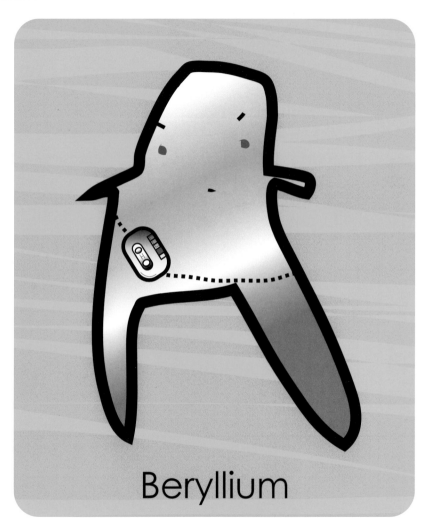
Beryllium

12 **Magnesium**

■ The Alkaline Earth Metals

- ✳ Symbol: Mg
- ✳ Atomic number: 12
- ✳ Atomic weight: 24.305
- ✳ Colour: Silver-white
- ✳ Standard state: Solid at 25 °C
- ✳ Classification: Metallic

I'm happy to mix in any social gathering of the elements, making friends with anyone, even moody Hydrogen. I am a sparky fellow and I always cause a reaction!

I'm a bit of a cheeky chappie, too – I can speed up your body processes and make you rush to the toilet! The laxatives Epsom salts and milk of magnesia are both made using my salts, which also give a bitter taste to food and can leave a bad taste in your mouth.

I am a silver-white metal and burn with incredible intensity and a bright white light. My splendiferous powers of combustion are used in flash bulbs, distress flares, fireworks and incendiary bombs. Strong and light, I help make bike frames, car parts and aircraft engines.

Date of discovery: 1755

- ● Density   1.738 g/cm^3
- ● Melting point   650 °C
- ● Boiling point   1090 °C

Magnesium

20 Calcium

■ The Alkaline Earth Metals

❋ Symbol: Ca
❋ Atomic number: 20
❋ Atomic weight: 40.078

❋ Colour: Silvery
❋ Standard state: Solid at 25 °C
❋ Classification: Metallic

They call me "The Scaffolder" because I make up a large portion of the bits that hold you together – your skeleton and teeth. I'm needed in large amounts as you grow, to build the calcium phosphate of your bones, and as you get older to keep your frame strong.

A reactive metal, I'm soft and silvery in appearance, but a bit of a hard man. When my ions dissolve in water it becomes "hard" – detergents won't lather, soap forms a surface scum and limescale forms in your kettle.

I've been known for centuries and am found in common compounds, such as lime, slaked lime, cement, chalk and limestone. All of these are white, have been used in construction and also have the ability to neutralize acid.

Date of discovery: 1808

● Density   1.550 g/cm³
● Melting point   842 °C
● Boiling point   1484 °C

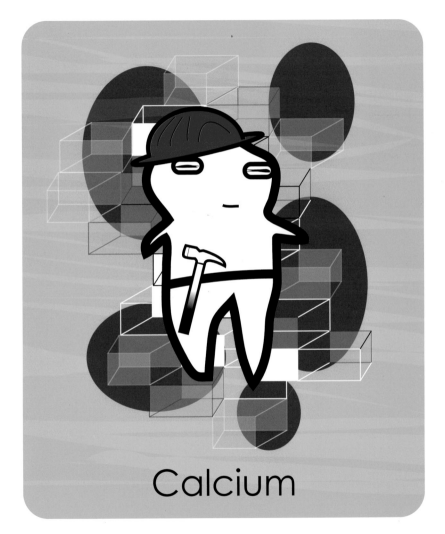

Calcium

38 **Strontium**

■ The Alkaline Earth Metals

- ✳ Symbol: Sr
- ✳ Atomic number: 38
- ✳ Atomic weight: 87.62
- ✳ Colour: Silvery
- ✳ Standard state: Solid at 25 °C
- ✳ Classification: Metallic

I'm a Scot, named after the town of Strontian where I was discovered. You may see me as a shy, run-of-the-mill silver-coloured metal, but I've got a few surprises up my sleeve. I'll catch your eye with the stunning crimson colours that I give to fireworks. Today, my main use is as an additive in the glass of TV sets and monitors.

My sneaky radioactive isotope, Strontium-90, has the eerie ability to mimic Calcium and get absorbed into growing bones. It releases harmful beta-particle radiation, which causes cancers. In the mid-twentieth century, testing of nuclear bombs meant that there was a lot of me about. I began to build up in the bodies of children… Luckily, the testing was stopped when scientists realised the potentially horrible consequences.

Date of discovery: 1790

- ● Density   2.630 g/cm³
- ● Melting point   777 °C
- ● Boiling point   1382 °C

Strontium

56 **Barium**

■ The Alkaline Earth Metals

- ✴ Symbol: Ba
- ✴ Atomic number: 56
- ✴ Atomic weight: 137.33

- ✴ Colour: Silver-white
- ✴ Standard state: Solid at 25 °C
- ✴ Classification: Metallic

One of the heavy metals, I'm a real rocker and more reactive than Calcium. My carbonate salt is a deadly rat poison, but my sulphate salt is insoluble and totally indigestible. It's used for "barium meals", which are neither tasty nor nutritious, but are ideal for seeing how you are digesting your food. When excited, my ions give off an apple-green colour.

Barium

Date of discovery: 1808

Ba
- ● Density — 3.510 g/cm³
- ● Melting point — 727 °C
- ● Boiling point — 1870 °C

Radium 88

The Alkaline Earth Metals ■

* Symbol: Ra
* Atomic number: 88
* Atomic weight: 226.03

* Colour: Silver-metallic
* Standard state: Solid at 25 °C
* Classification: Metallic

Radium

I am the heaviest of the gang and an utterly captivating character. I shine in any social situation. Bright and luminescent (I was used in luminous paint), I am a real stunner. I have the power to ionize air with the radioactive alpha particles I give off, creating a crackling bright blue aura around me.
My name comes from the Latin *radius*, meaning "ray".

Date of discovery: 1898

● Density   5.000 g/cm³
● Melting point   700 °C
● Boiling point   1737 °C

 Ra

CHAPTER 3
The Transition Elements

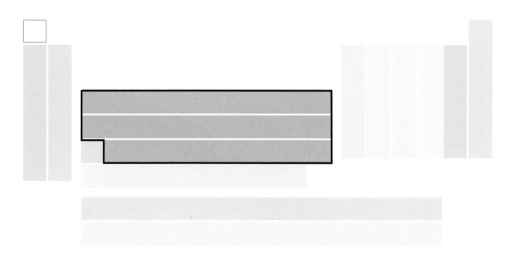

Stuck in the middle of the periodic table, the transition elements are a motley crew of roughnecks. Strapping, robust metals, these guys get involved in literally thousands of industrial applications. Many are movers and shakers, who kick-start all sorts of important manufacturing reactions. Others use their amazing ability to bond with a wide variety of other elements to form alloys – some of which have changed civilization for good. But it's not all grit and grime: the transition elements love to turn out in a dazzling variety of highly coloured forms.

21 **Sc** SCANDIUM

 22 **Ti** TITANIUM

 23 **V** VANADIUM

 24 **Cr** CHROMIUM

 25 **Mn** MANGANESE

 26 **Fe** IRON

 27 **Co** COBALT

 28 **Ni** NICKEL

 29 **Cu** COPPER

 30 **Zn** ZINC

 39 **Y** YTTRIUM

 40 **Zr** ZIRCONIUM

 41 **Nb** NIOBIUM

 42 **Mo** MOLYBDENUM

 43 **Tc** TECHNETIUM

 44 **Ru** RUTHENIUM

 45 **Rh** RHODIUM

 46 **Pd** PALLADIUM

 47 **Ag** SILVER

 48 **Cd** CADMIUM

 72 **Hf** HAFNIUM

 73 **Ta** TANTALUM

 74 **W** TUNGSTEN

 75 **Re** RHENIUM

 76 **Os** OSMIUM

 77 **Ir** IRIDIUM

 78 **Pt** PLATINUM

 79 **Au** GOLD

 80 **Hg** MERCURY

22 Titanium

The Transition Elements

* Symbol: Ti
* Atomic number: 22
* Atomic weight: 47.867

* Colour: Clean, gleaming silver
* Standard state: Solid at 25 °C
* Classification: Metallic

Titanium by name and a Titan by nature (Titans were strong, divine giants), I am brilliant, gleaming, extremely hard and very resistant to any kind of chemical attack.

As a dioxide compound (me plus two Oxygen atoms) I'm bright white and excellent at spreading myself about. This combo makes me king in the worlds of paint, paper, sunscreen, toothpaste, food dyes and also in enamelling and ceramic work.

My invulnerability makes me a favourite choice for bad-boy body piercings, but my main use is for super-hard metal alloys. These are used in aeroplane and spacecraft manufacture for their unrivalled combination of lightness and strength.

Date of discovery: 1791

● Density   4.507 g/cm³
● Melting point   1668 °C
● Boiling point   3287 °C

Titanium

23 **Vanadium**

■ The Transition Elements

* Symbol: V
* Atomic number: 23
* Atomic weight: 50.942

* Colour: Silver-grey
* Standard state: Solid at 25 °C
* Classification: Metallic

My beauty knows no bounds. I am named after the Scandinavian goddess of beauty and love, *Vanadis*. Depending on my state (the charge of my various ions), I can make a rainbow of brilliant and beautiful purple, green, blue and yellow solutions.

Like most transition metals, my colourful compounds can be used as catalysts (substances that allow chemical reactions to occur more freely). I am an essential catalyst in the "contact process" that is used to manufacture sulphuric acid, arguably the most important industrial chemical in the world today. I make up part of a crucial steel alloy that was used in Henry Ford's Model-T cars, so without me there may never have been a motor industry.

Date of discovery: 1801

● Density   6.110 g/cm³
● Melting point   1910 °C
● Boiling point   3407 °C

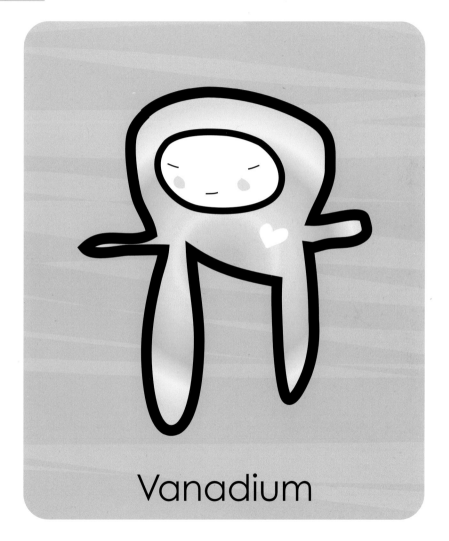

Vanadium

24 **Chromium**

■ The Transition Elements

* ✳ Symbol: Cr
* ✳ Atomic number: 24
* ✳ Atomic weight: 51.996
* ✳ Colour: Super-shiny silver
* ✳ Standard state: Solid at 25 °C
* ✳ Classification: Metallic

I'm a total flash geezer. You may know me as a shiny, decorative metal on bikes and fancy kitchen equipment, but I am much more than just a pretty face. My name comes from the Greek word *chroma*, which means "colour", because I can appear in an impressive range of funky shades (different oxidation states) from red to green, orange and yellow. I am responsible for the brilliant red colour of rubies and I put the "stainless" into stainless steel. There's no blemishing my record!

It's easy to take a shine to me – just polish me with a cloth. I'm almost completely resistant to corrosion. Because of this, I was once used as a protective layer (a plating) to stop steel surfaces rusting. I gave old cars their classic, mirrored-metal look. These days most cars use plastic.

Date of discovery: 1797

* ● Density — 7.140 g/cm³
* ● Melting point — 1907 °C
* ● Boiling point — 2671 °C

Cr

Chromium

25 Manganese

The Transition Elements

- ✳ Symbol: Mn
- ✳ Atomic number: 25
- ✳ Atomic weight: 54.938
- ✳ Colour: Silvery
- ✳ Standard state: Solid at 25 °C
- ✳ Classification: Metallic

I'm a hard and brittle element. I am found in large amounts in the rocks of the ocean floor and I'm most widely used in steel manufacture. Steel is much stronger when it is joined with me in an alloy.

Like many of the other transition metals, I can exist in many different forms (oxidation states) and I change my appearance like an undercover agent – I can be pink, black, green or dark purple.

Spend too long with me and I'll mess with your mind. I play an important role in the body, but too much of me can give you "manganese madness", a terrifying psychiatric condition that causes hallucinations. I have also been associated with Parkinson's disease.

Date of discovery: 1774

- ● Density   7.470 g/cm³
- ● Melting point   1246 °C
- ● Boiling point   2061 °C

Manganese

26 Iron

■ The Transition Elements

* ✹ Symbol: Fe
* ✹ Atomic number: 26
* ✹ Atomic weight: 55.845

* ✹ Colour: Grey
* ✹ Standard state: Solid at 25 °C
* ✹ Classification: Metallic

I am at the centre of everything. I am the hub. As the core element in your blood's haemoglobin – the substance that transports Oxygen around the body – I keep you alive. Journey to the centre of the Earth and you'll find me there at the core of things. I am the most abundant element in the planet you live on and I am at the heart of civilization, too.

I am the most important metal ever known to man. My use for tools and weapons transformed the ancient world; using me for construction and industrialization made the modern world. I'm most useful when I am mixed with small amounts of Carbon to produce steel. But I'm not without flaw – I oxidize easily when exposed to air and water, making rust a constant problem.

Earliest known use: c.2500BCE

* ● Density   7.874 g/cm³
* ● Melting point   1538 °C
* ● Boiling point   2861 °C

Iron

27 **Cobalt**

■ The Transition Elements

✸ Symbol: Co
✸ Atomic number: 27
✸ Atomic weight: 58.933

✸ Colour: Grey
✸ Standard state: Solid at 25 °C
✸ Classification: Metallic

Mysterious and attractive, I am the gremlin of the underworld. My name was given to me by German miners, who called me *kobald*, meaning "goblin". They thought I stopped them getting to other more valuable metals, such as Silver, and so believed my beautiful ores had been cursed by goblins.

For centuries my compounds have been used to add my distinctive and attractive colour to glass and objects. Although blue is my most well-known shade, green and pink are also prominent in my compounds.

My really useful radioactive isotope, Cobalt-60, is a powerful gamma-ray emitter used for radiotherapy, leak detection in pipes and irradiating food to kill bacteria.

Date of discovery: 1735

● Density   8.900 g/cm³
● Melting point   1495 °C
● Boiling point   2927 °C

Cobalt

28 Nickel

■ The Transition Elements

- ✳ Symbol: Ni
- ✳ Atomic number: 28
- ✳ Atomic weight: 58.693
- ✳ Colour: Silvery
- ✳ Standard state: Solid at 25 °C
- ✳ Classification: Metallic

Some people think of me as the devil in disguise because I'm often mistaken for Copper. My name is taken from the German word *kupfernickel*, meaning "devil's copper". Unfair! I'm really likeable and useful, too.

I love hanging out with the other transition metal elements and I'm great at forming alloys that make materials stronger and more resistant to corrosion. You'll find me in coins and charging around batteries, as well as in special heat-resistant materials. I am also used for plating car parts, as well as bathroom and kitchen fittings.

I make some exceptionally beautiful-coloured compounds and my favourite shade is green. But this beauty is only skin deep and I can bring people out in a nasty rash.

Date of discovery: 1751

- ● Density   8.908 g/cm³
- ● Melting point   1455 °C
- ● Boiling point   2913 °C

Nickel

29 **Copper**

The Transition Elements

* Symbol: Cu
* Atomic number: 29
* Atomic weight: 63.546

* Colour: Reddish
* Standard state: Solid at 25 °C
* Classification: Metallic

I am an age-old metal that gave birth to whole chunks of history and launched civilizations. As a pure metal or mixed with Tin to make bronze, I have been used for centuries to make ornaments and practical tools. Along with Tin, I formed the basis of the Bronze Age.

I am unique among metals in that I have a red hue, but some of my salts are a vivid blue. Indeed, many sea creatures have blue blood, because of my presence.

I'm the poor relation in a very well-to-do family. Along with Silver and Gold, we're known as the "coinage metals". However, these days I'm only used in "coppers" (along with Nickel). I am an exceptional conductor of electricity and heat, so I'm used in wiring and kettles.

Earliest known use: c.4500BCE

* Density   8.920 g/cm³
* Melting point   1084.62 °C
* Boiling point   2927 °C

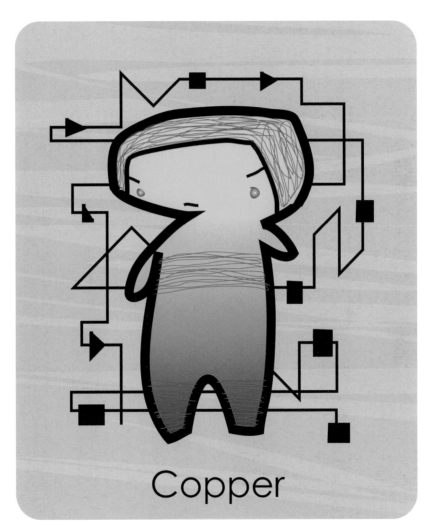

Copper

30 **Zinc**

▪ The Transition Elements

- ✴ Symbol: Zn
- ✴ Atomic number: 30
- ✴ Atomic weight: 65.409

- ✴ Colour: Bluish-grey
- ✴ Standard state: Solid at 25 °C
- ✴ Classification: Metallic

Here to protect and serve, I'm more useful than you'd ever zinc! I'm a very sociable element who's always happy to mix in with other metals. Brass is probably my most well-known alloy, formed when I get together with Copper. On my own I can be found in batteries.

With a thin layer of my atoms I "galvanize" steel, stopping water and oxygen from rusting it away. Even if I am scratched and the steel gets exposed, I quickly form zinc oxide before Iron in the steel has a chance to corrode. I also protect people from sunburn as the white zinc oxide sunblock that's ever-popular with cricketers.

What's more, I'm an essential element for loads of bodily processes and I can be taken as a dietary supplement.

Date of discovery: 1500

- ● Density — 7.140 g/cm³
- ● Melting point — 419.53 °C
- ● Boiling point — 907 °C

Zinc

42 **Molybdenum**

■ The Transition Elements

- ✳ Symbol: Mo
- ✳ Atomic number: 42
- ✳ Atomic weight: 95.94

- ✳ Colour: Grey
- ✳ Standard state: Solid at 25 °C
- ✳ Classification: Metallic

I am a real tough nut, so don't call me Molly. Add me to steel and it becomes super-resilient and heat-resistant. I am often found mixed up with lead ores, and my name even means "like lead". I am a friend to plants because I help them capture Nitrogen from the atmosphere for nutrition and get rid of any unwelcome Sulphur.

Molybdenum

Date of discovery: 1781

Mo
- ● Density — 10.280 g/cm³
- ● Melting point — 2623 °C
- ● Boiling point — 4639 °C

Palladium 46

The Transition Elements

* Symbol: Pd
* Atomic number: 46
* Atomic weight: 106.42

* Colour: Silvery
* Standard state: Solid at 25 °C
* Classification: Metallic

Palladium

I'm a wizard all around the industrial world because of my amazing skill as a catalyzer of reactions. This makes me even more sought-after than my close cousin Platinum. The secret lies in my surface pores. Hard at work in the catalytic converters of modern cars, I can potentially save the planet from harmful hydrocarbon emissions.

Date of discovery: 1803

● Density   12.023 g/cm³
● Melting point   1554.9 °C
● Boiling point   2963 °C

Pd

47 Silver

■ The Transition Elements

- ✸ Symbol: Ag
- ✸ Atomic number: 47
- ✸ Atomic weight: 107.87
- ✸ Colour: Silver
- ✸ Standard state: Solid at 25 °C
- ✸ Classification: Metallic

I'm as lustrous and luscious as a shining star! Whether made into money, jewellery or ornaments, I have always been coveted for my short-lived shininess. But I always lose out to Gold because I can't help forming silver sulphide when I come into contact with air. This forms a layer of black tarnish that needs to be cleaned off.

I'm soft and flexible, making me very easy to work with. Dentists use a little of me in so-called silver fillings (which are really mostly Mercury). My conductivity is first-rate, making me popular in electrical devices. However, I'm best known for my celluloid moments. As silver bromide and silver iodide I am incredibly sensitive to light. When these compounds are coated onto film they are great for capturing images – both photos and movies.

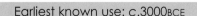

Earliest known use: c.3000BCE

- ● Density   10.490 g/cm³
- ● Melting point   961.78 °C
- ● Boiling point   2162 °C

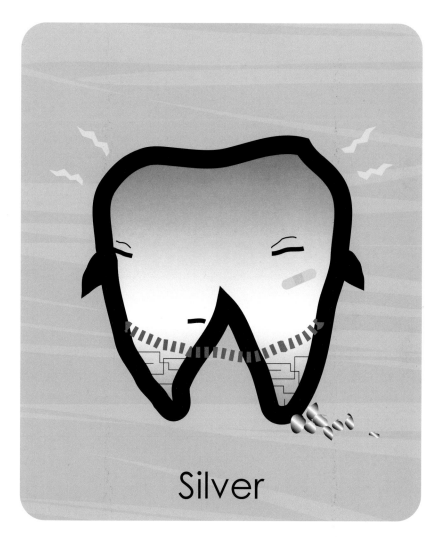

Silver

74 **Tungsten**

■ The Transition Elements

✳ Symbol: W
✳ Atomic number: 74
✳ Atomic weight: 183.84

✳ Colour: Grey-white
✳ Standard state: Solid at 25 °C
✳ Classification: Metallic

Call me "Wolfram" – that's my old-school alter ego and the reason for my surprising chemical symbol. I'm one tough cookie, with the highest melting point of all metals and a boiling point close to 6000 °C, so you'll find me hard to liquefy and boil. In fact, you'll find me just plain harder than nails!

My compound tungsten carbide will tear through anything like a knife through butter, so it's used to make high-speed cutting tools and drill bits. I am also used in golf clubs and balls, and fishing weights (I'm more dense and much less toxic than Lead). As the toughest of the tough, I can be found protecting soldiers as bullet-proof armour plating, but I still manage to bring light to the world in the filaments of light bulbs.

Date of discovery: 1783

● Density — 19.250 g/cm³
● Melting point — 3422 °C
● Boiling point — 5555 °C

Tungsten

78 **Platinum**

■ The Transition Elements

❋ Symbol: Pt
❋ Atomic number: 78
❋ Atomic weight: 195.08

❋ Colour: Silver-white
❋ Standard state: Solid at 25 °C
❋ Classification: Metallic

I'm the last word in good taste. Rarer and even more expensive than Gold, I am a bright, shiny metal found in South Africa and Russia. I am a real ladies' man, who is used to make jewellery and adored for my endlessly fascinating lustre. Steadfast and dependable, I never lose my shine because I'm resistant to corrosion.

One of my most valuable uses, like so many of my fellow transition metals, is as a catalyst getting things going in industrial reactions. As steady as they come, my ability to remain unchanged made me the natural choice for the standard kilogram mass – *Le Grand Kilo* – that is stored in Paris at the International Bureau of Weights and Measures. Another of my many and marvellous talents is being an essential component of anti-cancer drugs.

Date of discovery: 1735

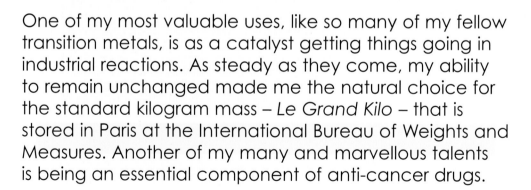

● Density   21.090 g/cm³
● Melting point   1768.3 °C
● Boiling point   3825 °C

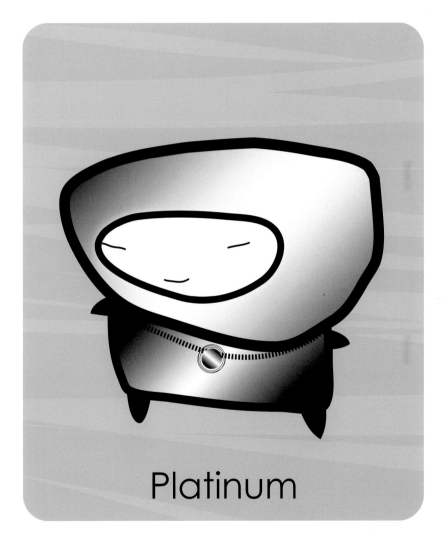

Platinum

79 **Gold**

■ The Transition Elements

- ✷ Symbol: Au
- ✷ Atomic number: 79
- ✷ Atomic weight: 196.97
- ✷ Colour: Gold
- ✷ Standard state: Solid at 25 °C
- ✷ Classification: Metallic

I am not the rarest or the most expensive element, but I am the world's most wanted. I am the original goldrush king, the ultimate attention seeker and a bling party boy! At heart, I'm soft (for a metal), which makes me very easy to work with, and I can be polished to a high shine. My attraction lies in my resistance to corrosion (oxidation), meaning I can be found in pure form in the earth. I always remain a glistening temptation.

I am found in jewellery, in most electronic equipment (I'm a sparkling conductor of electricity), as crowns on teeth, arthritis treatments and, of course, as solid-gold bullion. My purity is measured in carats – 24 carat is my purest form, but I can be alloyed (combined) with other metals to make 22-, 18-, 14- and 9-carat gold.

Earliest known use: c.3000BCE

- ● Density   19.300 g/cm³
- ● Melting point   1064.18 °C
- ● Boiling point   2856 °C

Gold

80 **Mercury**

■ The Transition Elements

- ✳ Symbol: Hg
- ✳ Atomic number: 80
- ✳ Atomic weight: 200.59

- ✳ Colour: Silvery
- ✳ Standard state: Liquid at 25 °C
- ✳ Classification: Metallic

Quick and deadly, that's me. I put the "mad" in Mad Hatter and my ability to poison the brain is legendary! A sinister, silver-coloured killer, I am a strange and stealthy liquid metal that easily vapourizes into toxic fumes. Most of the forms I take are lethal – hat makers who used mercury nitrate for their work often succumbed to a weird delirium called "mercury madness".

I tend to build up in the bodies of animals, especially in fish that swim in waters polluted by me. I attack the nervous systems of those who eat the contaminated fish. Alchemists mistakenly thought of me as the key for converting base metals into Gold, and I was once very useful in mining and for filling tooth cavities, but health and safety rules mean I'm not used widely any more.

Earliest known use: c.1500BCE

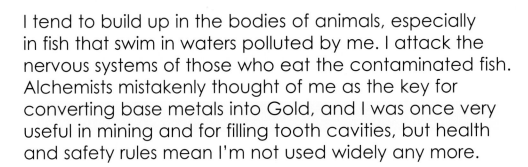

- ● Density   13.534 g/cm³
- ● Melting point   −38.83 °C
- ● Boiling point   356.73 °C

Mercury

CHAPTER 4

The Boron Elements

Group III

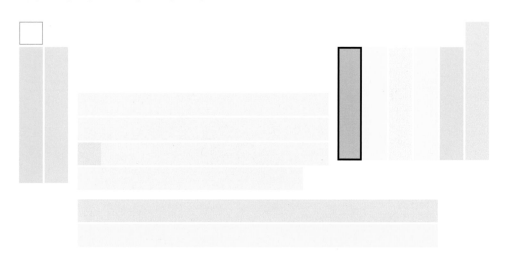

This ragbag group of elements are the periodic table's dysfunctional family. They don't gel together – some of them aren't even the same type of substance! Lonely, odd-man-out Boron is an unusual powdery non-metal, whereas the rest are soft, silvery and weak metals.
At the top of the group, these metals aren't particularly metallic, but the further down the group you go, the more like metals the members get. The boron elements are reactive enough to form many different compounds and are found in nature as various minerals and ores.

5

B

BORON

13

Al

ALUMINIUM

31

Ga

GALLIUM

49

In

INDIUM

81

Tl

THALLIUM

5 Boron

■ The Boron Elements

- ☀ Symbol: B
- ☀ Atomic number: 5
- ☀ Atomic weight: 10.811
- ☀ Colour: Browny-black
- ☀ Standard state: Solid at 25 °C
- ☀ Classification: Non-metallic

People make fun of my name and call me "Boring Boron". OK, so I'm not flamboyant and I dress in browns and blacks, but I'm really good to have around. I'm a facilitator and a helpful element, who gets things done – a self-starter, if I could be so bold.

Whether helping out in glass manufacture, in detergents or – in my guise as borax and boric acid – coaxing along chemical reactions in industry, I'm on the job. My compound boron nitrate is nearly as hard as diamond.

Far from tedious, you can think of me as a maverick. I am quite literally the "black-brown sheep" of the boron element family, since I'm the only non-metal amongst my metallic mates.

Date of discovery: 1808

- ● Density   2.460 g/cm³
- ● Melting point   2076 °C
- ● Boiling point   3927 °C

Boron

13 Aluminium

■ The Boron Elements

- ❋ Symbol: Al
- ❋ Atomic number: 13
- ❋ Atomic weight: 26.982

- ❋ Colour: Silver-grey
- ❋ Standard state: Solid at 25 °C
- ❋ Classification: Metallic

I'm light on my feet, and my pocket-battleship strength has made me a powerhouse metal. As a featherweight, I quite literally punch well above my weight! I offer a superior blend of strength and lightness – you can make me into aeroplanes, "tin" cans, foil and beer kegs.

I am the third most abundant element in the world, but you have to work hard to get to me. I bind tightly to my ore, bauxite, and extracting me takes a huge amount of electrical power.

My salts help purify water by causing impurities to drop out of solution as solids, but they have been linked to poisoning. When I show up in tap water, I have turned people's hair green and caused brain disorders.

Date of discovery: 1825

- ● Density — 2.700 g/cm³
- ● Melting point — 660.32 °C
- ● Boiling point — 2519 °C

Aluminium

CHAPTER 5

The Carbon Elements

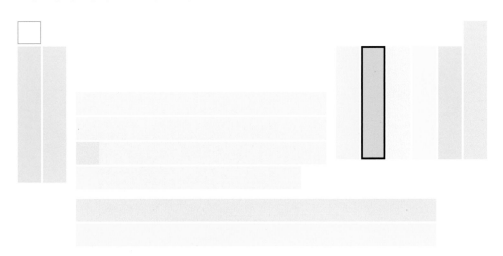

Unpredictability hangs like a conjuror's cloak over this group of tricky chemicals. This group has very few striking similarities. Carbon is a hard (and even sometimes transparent) non-metal, whereas Tin and Lead are softer metals. Like Group III, the carbon elements get more metallic towards the bottom of the table. The members form a bewildering variety of different compounds so perhaps it would be better to consider each element as an individual, rather than as part of a collection of like-minded substances.

6

C

CARBON

14

Si

SILICON

32

Ge

GERMANIUM

50

Sn

TIN

82

Pb

LEAD

6 **Carbon**

The Carbon Elements

* Symbol: C
* Atomic number: 6
* Atomic weight: 12.011
* Colour: Black
* Standard state: Solid at 25 °C
* Classification: Non-metallic

Hah-yah! Wherever you look, I'm there. Like a ninja, there's no escaping me! A master of the black arts, I'm a stealthy element and can morph into many forms – black charcoal, hard and brilliant diamonds, slippery graphite and lovely balls of buckminsterfullerene. My contortionist's ability to form several types of chemical bond with myself means that I can whip myself into all sorts of shapes. With so many different guises, there's a whole branch of "organic" chemistry devoted to me.

I form the bulk of all living matter. Almost everything you eat – fats, sugars and fibre – is a carbon-based compound. I move about the food chain in what's called "The Carbon Cycle". I'm released from food in breath and body waste, absorbed by plants and eaten again.

No known date of discovery

* Density   2.267 g/cm³
* Melting point   3527 °C
* Boiling point   4027 °C

Carbon

14 Silicon

The Carbon Elements

- Symbol: Si
- Atomic number: 14
- Atomic weight: 28.086

- Colour: Glassy off-white
- Standard state: Solid at 25 °C
- Classification: Non-metallic

My beguiling charms make computers run and power the digital age. Combined with Boron or Phosphorus, I become a semi-conducting sorcerer. These special powers gave birth to the silicon chip and the Computer Age. Silicon Valley is named after me.

I can take many different forms. As the second most abundant element on Earth, you can find me as sand, quartz, flint and countless other minerals. As the famous silicone (a long chain made up of me, Oxygen and organic groups), I turn up in lubricants and adhesives.

In glass, I'm perfectly clear. In quartz watches and clocks, I keep time, while as silica gel, I keep products moisture-free. You'll find me in sachets, in boxes of electrical goods.

Date of discovery: 1824

- Density   2.330 g/cm³
- Melting point   1414 °C
- Boiling point   2900 °C

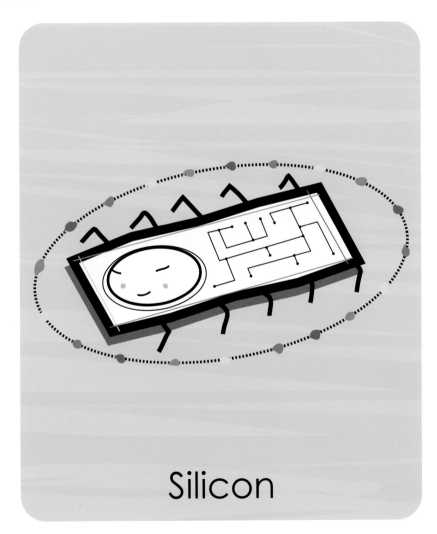

Silicon

50 Tin

■ The Carbon Elements

- ✳ Symbol: Sn
- ✳ Atomic number: 50
- ✳ Atomic weight: 118.71

- ✳ Colour: Dull silver
- ✳ Standard state: Solid at 25 °C
- ✳ Classification: Metallic

I am a wily old metal with a long and distinguished history. Starting way back in the Bronze Age, I have been the ultimate mixer for metals. My most notable alloys are pewter (mingled with Copper and Bismuth), solder (teamed up with Lead) and, of course, bronze (my ancient and long-lived partnership with Copper).

I am too soft for my own good – in fact, I can be shaped with very little effort. But my problem is that I melt at a low temperature (for a metal) and below 13 °C, I change from a solid into a crumbly powder. I get mixed with other metals to keep me in shape. (I'm only a thin coating on "tin cans" – they're actually made of Aluminium or steel.) The "Pilkington process" produces pancake-flat glass, by floating molten glass onto a surface of me in liquid form.

Earliest known use: c.3500BCE

- ● Density   7.310 g/cm³
- ● Melting point   231.93 °C
- ● Boiling point   2602 °C

Tin

82 Lead

■ The Carbon Elements

- ✳ Symbol: Pb
- ✳ Atomic number: 82
- ✳ Atomic weight: 207.2

- ✳ Colour: Dull, dark grey
- ✳ Standard state: Solid at 25 °C
- ✳ Classification: Metallic

Don't let my heavyweight status fool you – at heart I'm a totally malleable softie. I am so easy to work with that the ancient Romans used me for their water pipes. My chemical symbol (and the word "plumbing") comes from my Latin name *plumbum*.

Over the years, I've gained a bad rep. They say I build up in bones as a slow poison and that I have damaged kids' development. It's true I have an unfortunate ability to slip easily into the food chain – from pipes and cookware, leaded petrol and paints to fishermen's weights. I have also been blamed for ending the ancient Roman civilization. Not fair! These days I am closely regulated. But I am still used as a shield against X-rays, for roofing and stained glass.

No known date of discovery

- ● Density   11.340 g/cm³
- ● Melting point   327.46 °C
- ● Boiling point   1749 °C

Lead

CHAPTER 6
The Nitrogen Elements

Group V

The "Pnictogens" (nick-toe-jens), as they are sometimes (but rarely) called, are an ancient and alchemical lot with an odd collection of properties to boot. The group is a real mishmash of matter – there are metals, non-metals, strange metalloids; several elements exist in two different guises, and there's a mixture of gases and solids thrown in for good measure. Like most groups in the periodic table, the elements of Group V get increasingly metallic towards the base. Nitrogen is a colourless gas, whereas Bismuth is a brittle metal.

7

N

NITROGEN

15

P

PHOSPHORUS

33

As

ARSENIC

51

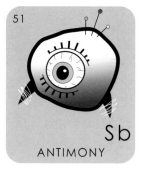

Sb

ANTIMONY

83

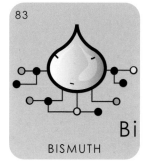

Bi

BISMUTH

7 Nitrogen

The Nitrogen Elements

* Symbol: N
* Atomic number: 7
* Atomic weight: 14.007
* Colour: None
* Standard state: Gas at 25 °C
* Classification: Non-metallic

On first impressions I'm a regular guy, but I've got an explosive temperament. You might hardly notice me, but I make up nearly 80 per cent of air and I'm essential to plant life on Earth.

I'm normally a pretty unreactive gas, made up of two atoms of nitrogen (N_2). The triple bond between these two atoms is hard to break, and that is my hidden power. When nitrogen atoms form nitrogen gas, they release massive amounts of energy. This makes many compounds that contain me potentially explosive!

I'm very easy to extract from air. I am a spectacular coolant in liquid form. At close to −200 °C, I will freeze almost anything that comes into contact with me.

Date of discovery: 1772

* Density   1.145 g/l
* Melting point   −210.10 °C
* Boiling point   −195.79 °C

N

Nitrogen

15 **Phosphorus**

The Nitrogen Elements

* Symbol: P
* Atomic number: 15
* Atomic weight: 30.974

* Colour: Black, red or white
* Standard state: Solid at 25 °C
* Classification: Non-metallic

Like anything intriguing, I'm hard to pin down. I'm a Jekyll & Hyde element – essential to life, yet wickedly dangerous at the same time – a chameleon who appears in black, red or white. I play a pivotal part in the DNA molecule and in the body, but I can be deadly. My white form ignites in air and even burns underwater! I can inflict terrible burns and sadly I was used for that purpose in World War II. I am a central element in sarin – a lethal nerve gas used in the 1995 attack on the subway in Tokyo, Japan.

Arguably my most important use is in fertilizers. I am also used in many foods as phosphoric acid (an acidifying agent). You can find me in any bottle of cola, which is why you can use those fizzy drinks as a rust remover.

Date of discovery: 1669

* Density — 1.823 g/cm³
* Melting point — 44.2 °C
* Boiling point — 277 °C

Phosphorus

33 **Arsenic**

■ The Nitrogen Elements

* ☀ Symbol: As
* ☀ Atomic number: 33
* ☀ Atomic weight: 74.922

* ☀ Colour: Grey or yellow
* ☀ Standard state: Solid at 25 °C
* ☀ Classification: Metalloid

Make no mistake – I am a deadly element. A murderer's delight and a master of disguise to boot! One minute I'm a grey-coloured metal, the next a yellow-coloured non-metal, and my furtive ability to hide with ease and avoid detection makes me a favourite choice of the poisoner.

Since I've got the properties of both a metal and a non-metal, I'm known as a metalloid. I wreak havoc in developing countries where industrial pollution allows me to sneak into the drinking water.

Contamination with me causes widespread health issues, but very small amounts of me are actually essential. You eat more of me than you'd care to know, with no ill effect – mainly in seafood such as shrimps.

Earliest known use: c.1250

* ● Density   5.727 g/cm³
* ● Melting point   817 °C
* ● Boiling point   614 °C

Arsenic

51 **Antimony**

■ The Nitrogen Elements

- ✳ Symbol: Sb
- ✳ Atomic number: 51
- ✳ Atomic weight: 121.76

- ✳ Colour: Silver-grey
- ✳ Standard state: Solid at 25 °C
- ✳ Classification: Metalloid

A curious and ancient metalloid, I am often found attached to other elements. Keep an eye out for me – although I'm used in mascara, I can induce violent vomiting and certain death. Like my buddy Arsenic, I was once popular among those with murder in mind. Today, I'm more often used to make alloys and semi-conductors.

Antimony

No known date of discovery

Sb

- ● Density   6.697 g/cm³
- ● Melting point   630.63 °C
- ● Boiling point   1587 °C

Bismuth 83

The Nitrogen Elements ▪

* Symbol: Bi
* Atomic number: 83
* Atomic weight: 208.98

* Colour: Silver-white
* Standard state: Solid at 25 °C
* Classification: Metalloid

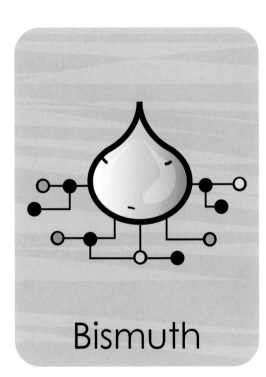

Bismuth

People tend to confuse me with Tin or Lead, which bugs me. I'm special too! I am the heaviest non-radioactive element. Others may decay to form more durable elements giving off radiation, but I'm stable. Because I turn into a liquid easily, I am used as part of fire-alarm circuits. When I melt in intense heat, it triggers the alarms and water sprinklers.

No known date of discovery

● Density   9.780 g/cm³
● Melting point   271.3 °C
● Boiling point   1564 °C

Bi

CHAPTER 7
The Oxygen Elements

Group VI

In this neighbourhood of the periodic table, the groups of elements are more like bunches of mates than family units. Nothing is truer for Group VI – it's a real mixed bag of solids, gases, non-metals, metalloids and even a radioactive metal – but the oxygen elements are a cosmopolitan crew, who get involved in important industrial reactions and are vital to many life processes. They sport the unlikely name "The Chalcogens", which means "ore former", because in nature they are often found combined with metals.

8

OXYGEN

O

16

SULPHUR

S

34

SELENIUM

Se

52

TELLURIUM

Te

84

POLONIUM

Po

8 Oxygen

The Oxygen Elements

* ✹ Symbol: O
* ✹ Atomic number: 8
* ✹ Atomic weight: 15.999

* ✹ Colour: None
* ✹ Standard state: Gas at 25 °C
* ✹ Classification: Non-metallic

Quiet and unassuming, I'm colourless, odourless and tasteless. Some say I lack personality, but they don't recognize true greatness. I am the powerhouse behind most chemical reactions on Earth. Without *me*, you die.

I'm a gas made up of two atoms (O_2), which combines readily with other substances in "oxidation reactions" to release energy. When you breathe me in, I slip into your bloodstream. Once I'm inside, every single cell uses me to fuel life-sustaining chemical reactions.

I am also found in teams of three atoms (O_3) as a gas known as ozone. When I take this form high in the sky, I protect Earth from the Sun's harmful ultraviolet rays.

Date of discovery: 1774

* ● Density   1.308 g/l
* ● Melting point   −218.3 °C
* ● Boiling point   −182.9 °C

Oxygen

16 **Sulphur**

The Oxygen Elements

* Symbol: S
* Atomic number: 16
* Atomic weight: 32.065
* Colour: Pale yellow
* Standard state: Solid at 25 °C
* Classification: Non-metallic

Sweetly smiling and dressed in pale yellow, I look as harmless as a custard tart, but I have a wicked side... I am a fun-loving prankster, who loves to unleash bad smells. My nastiest whiffs include rotten eggs and foul skunky odours. But it's not really me, it's my compounds that stink – hydrogen sulphide (H_2S) is the most likely culprit.

I was once known as "brimstone" and featured in fiery descriptions of Hell. This reputation probably comes from the fact that I ooze from the pores of active volcanoes. When exposed to Oxygen and heated, I spontaneously combust with a bright and intense light. These qualities make me an important part of gunpowder. I also cause acid rain. I am an essential element in sulphuric acid – a chemical used to make a multitude of other substances.

No known date of discovery

* Density — 1.960 g/cm³
* Melting point — 115.21 °C
* Boiling point — 444.72 °C

Sulphur

34 **Selenium**

■ The Oxygen Elements

* ✸ Symbol: Se
* ✸ Atomic number: 34
* ✸ Atomic weight: 78.96

* ✸ Colour: Grey
* ✸ Standard state: Solid at 25 °C
* ✸ Classification: Non-metallic

My name comes from the Greek word *selene*, meaning "moon" – I am a remote and mysterious element. Absence of me in your diet gives you Keshan disease, which causes heart muscle failure. But when animals eat me concentrated in plants such as vetch (aka "loco weed"), I make them stagger around as if they were drunk!

Selenium

Date of discovery: 1817

Se
* ● Density — 4.819 g/cm³
* ● Melting point — 221 °C
* ● Boiling point — 685 °C

Tellurium 52
The Oxygen Elements

* Symbol: Te
* Atomic number: 52
* Atomic weight: 127.60

* Colour: Silver-grey
* Standard state: Solid at 25 °C
* Classification: Semi-metal

Tellurium

Although useful in electronics, I'm a right problem child. I've been a puzzle since day one and identifying and classifying me has been a dizzying quandary. As a corrupting influence I am without equal. I'm about the only compound that can touch the spotless Gold. In the body I cause extremely bad breath, as well as nasty BO.

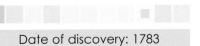

Date of discovery: 1783

* Density   6.240 g/cm³
* Melting point   449.51 °C
* Boiling point   988 °C

Te

CHAPTER 8
The Halogen Elements

Group VII

We're back in the family zone again, but on this side of the periodic table live the non-metal elements, separated from the metals to their left. The halogens are a close-knit group of lively, strongly coloured non-metals. They are a feisty bunch, who will react violently with metals to form salts (halogen means "salt giver"). The elements at the top of Group VII are yellow and green toxic gases, but as you move down through the group, things get progressively darker...

9

F

FLUORINE

17

Cl

CHLORINE

35

Br

BROMINE

53

I

IODINE

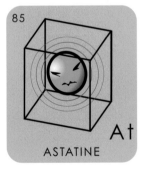

85

At

ASTATINE

9 Fluorine

The Halogen Elements

- Symbol: F
- Atomic number: 9
- Atomic weight: 18.998
- Colour: Pale yellow/green
- Standard state: Gas at 25 °C
- Classification: Non-metallic

I'm a doer – a lively package, set off by the perfect Hollywood smile. I am added to drinking water to help protect your teeth, and I form loads of really useful compounds, such as Teflon®, the famous non-stick coating. Running through all the wonderful things I do is a competitive streak. I am super-reactive and I will take an electron from nearly any atom or molecule to complete my set. This is just one of the reasons why I'm so usable and form so many nifty compounds.

The only blot on my copybook is my involvement with CFCs (chlorofluorocarbons) – the compounds that have done so much damage to the Earth's ozone layer. I don't like to talk about it. My invasive choking smell signals my true toxic nature. So be warned!

Date of discovery: 1886

- Density 1.553 g/l
- Melting point −219.62 °C
- Boiling point −188.12 °C

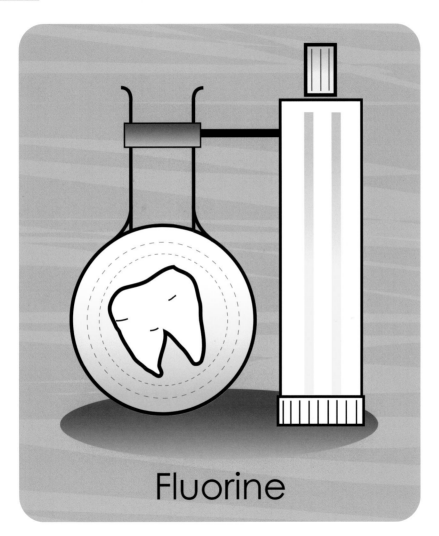

Fluorine

17 Chlorine

The Halogen Elements

- ✴ Symbol: Cl
- ✴ Atomic number: 17
- ✴ Atomic weight: 35.453

- ✴ Colour: Green
- ✴ Standard state: Gas at 25 °C
- ✴ Classification: Non-metallic

You've gotta give me respect! I'm a mean, green killing machine. One of the halogen gang, I'm a toxic gas with a nasty history. I first became a terrifying chemical weapon during World War I, where my sinister, choking fumes killed thousands. I'm bad enough even to battle bacteria in the toilet bowl! But I can also keep you safe from water-borne diseases, such as cholera and typhoid. Adding small amounts of me to drinking water supplies has saved millions of people's lives.

Usually obtained from common salt, you'll find me in all sorts of places, from salt shakers to swimming pools (where I keep the water bacteria-free). I have also been used as a particularly un-environmentally friendly pesticide called DDT and am associated with CFCs (see Fluorine).

Date of discovery: 1774

- ● Density   2.898 g/l
- ● Melting point   −101.5 °C
- ● Boiling point   −34.04 °C

Chlorine

35 **Bromine**

■ The Halogen Elements

* ❋ Symbol: Br
* ❋ Atomic number: 35
* ❋ Atomic weight: 79.904

* ❋ Colour: Orangey-brown
* ❋ Standard state: Liquid at 25 °C
* ❋ Classification: Non-metallic

I am a regal element with a long history. One of just two liquids in the periodic table (the other is Mercury), I was used in the royal dye of the ancient Roman empire – "Tyrian purple". Made from crushed seashells, emperors and members of the imperial family wore me proudly, to show everyone else how important they were.

Today, I am extracted from sea water and as an element you'll find me a pungent-smelling, red-brown, volatile liquid. I'm ashamed to say that my name comes from the Greek word *bromos*, meaning "stench".

Until recently, doctors used my salts to suppress mental activity in disturbed patients, but not any more since their toxic nature has been revealed.

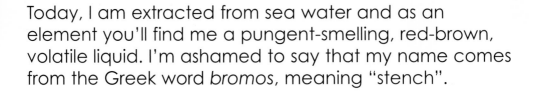

Date of discovery: 1826

* ● Density   3.1028 g/cm³
* ● Melting point   −7.3 °C
* ● Boiling point   59 °C

Bromine

53 Iodine

■ The Halogen Elements

- ✳ Symbol: I
- ✳ Atomic number: 53
- ✳ Atomic weight: 126.90

- ✳ Colour: Shiny black
- ✳ Standard state: Solid at 25 °C
- ✳ Classification: Non-metallic

Appearances can be deceptive – I am a shiny black solid, but at room temperature I often change into a purplish gas. That's called "sublimation".

You'll almost never see me alone – I hang out in pairs as a gas (I_2). I am deadly to bacteria when I'm in solution. I am a yellow-brown liquid that stings like heck when it gets dabbed onto a cut (although this may be the fault of the liquid alcohol). My antiseptic powers are so good, I'm used to clean up inside the body after surgery.

I've been sneaking into the diet for many years disguised in table salt, but that's a good thing – I help to eliminate the horrible swellings of the neck that used to affect people who didn't have enough of me in their bodies.

Date of discovery: 1811

- ● Density   4.940 g/cm³
- ● Melting point   113.7 °C
- ● Boiling point   184.3 °C

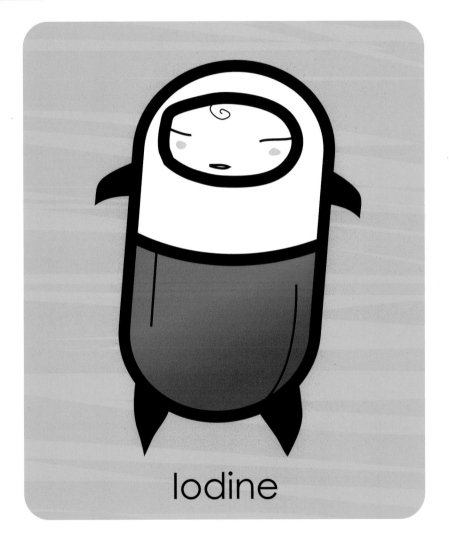

Iodine

CHAPTER 9

The Noble Gases

The far right of the table is the classy neighbourhood, for here lives the periodic table's royal family – the so-called "noble gases". This group is largely resistant to chemical reaction, seemingly above mixing or slumming it with the rest of the elements. They were once called the "inert gases", meaning completely unreactive, but this isn't entirely true – some of them have been caught in clandestine clinches with other elements. They're not even that rare either – we now know that they all float about in the atmosphere, alone and aloof.

2

He

HELIUM

10

Ne

NEON

18

Ar

ARGON

36

Kr

KRYPTON

54

Xe

XENON

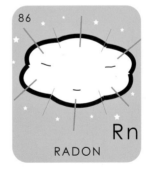

86

Rn

RADON

2 Helium

The Noble Gases

* Symbol: He
* Atomic number: 2
* Atomic weight: 4.0026

* Colour: None
* Standard state: Gas at 25 °C
* Classification: Non-metallic

I prefer my own company, thank you very much. Some call me aloof, but I'm happy not to mix with the riff-raff of the periodic table. I am a "noble" gas – the very first. I am utterly inert with no colour, taste or smell. I am also known as a bit of a party prankster. Gulp me from a birthday balloon and your voice will go all squeaky!

I am produced in massive stars like the Sun, where four hydrogen atoms fuse together, releasing ginormous amounts of energy. On Earth, my nucleus is one of the products of radioactive decay – the alpha particle.

My main uses are in weather balloons and airships – which need my lofty, lighter-than-air properties – and welding, which requires an inert, unreactive atmosphere.

Date of discovery: 1895

* Density   0.164 g/l
* Melting point   −272.2 °C
* Boiling point   −268.93 °C

Helium

10 **Neon**

■ The Noble Gases

* Symbol: Ne
* Atomic number: 10
* Atomic weight: 20.18

* Colour: None
* Standard state: Gas at 25 °C
* Classification: Non-metallic

I must be the funkiest element around. My name is derived from the Greek word *neos*, which means "new". (Maybe any new element could have been christened this way, but I think it suits me very well.) Things really get going when I become excited by electrical energy – my electrons zap and zing, and make me emit bright, brilliant and stunningly coloured red light. When other elements are stirred into the mix I can produce all the colours of the rainbow. This is how neon lights are made.

Even though I am found in something as common as air, I am a member of the periodic table's aristocracy – the noble gases. I keep myself to myself. I am a colourless, odourless and tasteless gas, and there is virtually nothing that I will react with.

Date of discovery: 1898

● Density   0.825 g/l
● Melting point   −248.59 °C
● Boiling point   −246.08 °C

Neon

18 **Argon**

The Noble Gases

* Symbol: Ar
* Atomic number: 18
* Atomic weight: 39.948

* Colour: None
* Standard state: Gas at 25 °C
* Classification: Non-metallic

Bone idle and basically lazy, I'm totally lacklustre – an odourless, colourless and tasteless gas, but don't call me a good-for-nothing. I'm renowned for my unwillingness and inability to react with anything at all! This can be a good thing – I am used as an "inert atmosphere" in potentially dangerous jobs, such as arc welding, when Oxygen must be excluded to avoid explosions. I am also sometimes used in light bulbs. You can even find me between the panes of double-glazed windows because I am such a poor conductor of heat.

As the third most abundant gas in the Earth's atmosphere, I'm extracted from liquid air. Because I am produced when the radioactive isotope Potassium-40 decays, my presence in the atmosphere is increasing with time.

Date of discovery: 1894

* Density   1.633 g/l
* Melting point   −189.3 °C
* Boiling point   −185.8 °C

Argon

36 **Krypton**

■ The Noble Gases

- ✹ Symbol: Kr
- ✹ Atomic number: 36
- ✹ Atomic weight: 83.798

- ✹ Colour: None
- ✹ Standard state: Gas at 25 °C
- ✹ Classification: Non-metallic

I'm elusive to say the least! My name, from the Greek *kryptos*, means "hidden", and it is aptly chosen. I'm almost completely unreactive, colourless, odourless, tasteless and only present in the atmosphere in vanishingly small amounts. Don't confuse me with the fictional home planet of Superman and the source of his nemesis – kryptonite!

Krypton

Date of discovery: 1898

Kr

- ● Density   3.425 g/l
- ● Melting point   −157.36 °C
- ● Boiling point   −153.22 °C

Radon 86
The Noble Gases ■

* Symbol: Rn
* Atomic number: 86
* Atomic weight: 222.02

* Colour: None
* Standard state: Gas at 25 °C
* Classification: Non-metallic

Radon

Like my other "noble" family members, I'm almost completely immune to chemical reactions, but I'm a much more sparky character than the rest. I give off harmful radioactive alpha particles and, since I occur in granite, there is concern that I may build up inside houses in granitic areas and pose a risk of lung cancer.

Date of discovery: 1900

● Density — 9.074 g/l
● Melting point — −71 °C
● Boiling point — −61.7 °C

Rn

CHAPTER 10
The Lanthanides and Actinides

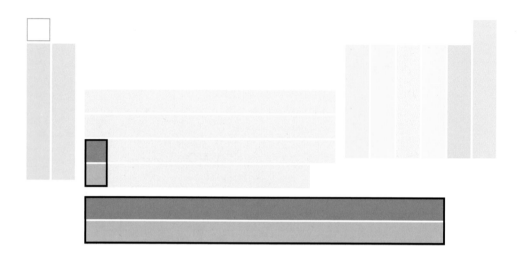

Removed from the main body of the periodic table, the lanthanides and actinides are outcasts. Sometimes called the "f-block" elements, they are a loosely grouped bunch of misfits. The lanthanides are naturally occurring heavy metals, used to date the rocks from outer space and widely used in lasers. The actinides are all dangerously radioactive elements. Only two of them are naturally occurring – the rest are produced in nuclear reactors and particle accelerators, and decay (break down) in the blink of an eye.

57 | La | LANTHANUM

58 | Ce | CERIUM

59 | Pr | PRASEODYMIUM

60 | Nd | NEODYMIUM

61 | Pm | PROMETHIUM

62 | Sm | SAMARIUM

63 | Eu | EUROPIUM

64 | Gd | GADOLINIUM

65 | Tb | TERBIUM

66 | Dy | DYSPROSIUM

67 | Ho | HOLMIUM

68 | Er | ERBIUM

69 | Tm | THULIUM

70 | Yb | YTTERBIUM

71 | Lu | LUTETIUM

89 | Ac | ACTINIUM

90 | Th | THORIUM

91 | Pa | PROTACTINIUM

92 | U | URANIUM

93 | Np | NEPTUNIUM

94 | Pu | PLUTONIUM

95 | Am | AMERICIUM

96 | Cm | CURIUM

97 | Bk | BERKELIUM

98 | Cf | CALIFORNIUM

99 | Es | EINSTEINIUM

100 | Fm | FERMIUM

101 | Md | MENDELEVIUM

102 | No | NOBELIUM

103 | Lr | LAWRENCIUM

92 **Uranium**

■ The Lanthanides and Actinides

❋ Symbol: U
❋ Atomic number: 92
❋ Atomic weight: 238.03

❋ Colour: Grey
❋ Standard state: Solid at 25 °C
❋ Classification: Metallic

I am a force of nature – one of the most powerful elements and the one with the greatest impact on history. My secret lies within my nucleus and the key is simple but deadly. Take a neutron and fire it at my unstable, radioactive form (atomic number 235). My nucleus splits apart with a roar of energy, firing neutrons in all directions. These go on to split other nuclei as I allow the chain reaction to rip me apart!

When this mighty reaction (called nuclear fission) is controlled in nuclear reactors, it can be used to generate power, but pack me into a bomb and I cause chaos. I can flatten whole cities. In 1945, an atomic bomb made of me was dropped on Hiroshima, Japan, with horrific results – signalling the start of the Atomic Age.

Date of discovery: 1789

● Density   19.050 g/cm³
● Melting point   1132.2 °C
● Boiling point   3927 °C

Uranium

94 Plutonium

■ The Lanthanides and Actinides

* ✳ Symbol: Pu
* ✳ Atomic number: 94
* ✳ Atomic weight: 244.06
* ✳ Colour: Silver-white
* ✳ Standard state: Solid at 25 °C
* ✳ Classification: Metallic

Unlike that Disney dog, life ain't no cartoon for me –
I'm deadly serious. Born in Berkeley, California, in 1941,
I was made by nuclear scientists, who named me
after the dwarf planet, Pluto. My nucleus was soon
the centre of attention. In August 1945, a nuclear
bomb made from my "239" isotope was dropped on
the Japanese city of Nagasaki. It killed or injured close
to 200,000 people and effectively ended World War II.

Although I'm dull to look at, inside I'm hot stuff. A lump
of me radiates heat because of the enormous amount
of radioactive alpha particles I release. I'm still closely
guarded because of my bomb-making potential but
I can be used for peaceful purposes, too. I am
a by-product of nuclear power plants.

Date of discovery: 1940

* ● Density 19.816 g/cm³
* ● Melting point 639.4 °C
* ● Boiling point 3230 °C

Plutonium

CHAPTER 11
The Transactinides

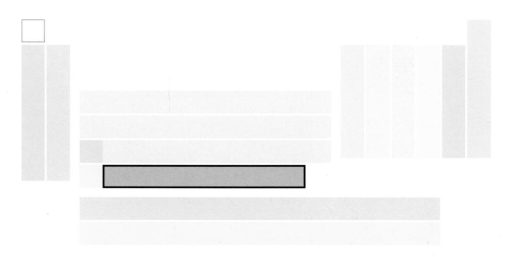

This group is totally "out there". Here at the far reaches of the periodic table live elements with atomic numbers greater than 103. These super-heavy substances have all been artificially created in the lab, so most of them have only ever existed in minuscule amounts. Every single one is extremely radioactive and decays incredibly quickly. Many labs all around the world lay claim to having been the first to produce the elements, so there is always a great deal of healthy argument over what each element should be called.

104

Rf

RUTHERFORDIUM

105

Db

DUBNIUM

106

Sg

SEABORGIUM

107

Bh

BOHRIUM

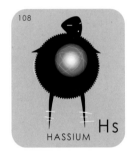

108

Hs

HASSIUM

109

Mt

MEITNERIUM

110

Ds

DARMSTADTIUM

111

Rg

ROENTGENIUM

INDEX

A
actinides	118
alkali metals	10
alkaline earth metals	20
Aluminium	68
Antimony	88
Argon	114
Arsenic	86

B
Barium	30
Beryllium	22
Bismuth	89
Boron	66
boron elements	64
Bromine	104
Bronze Age	48, 76

C
Caesium	19
Calcium	26
Carbon	72
carbon elements	70
Chalcogens	90
Chlorine	102
Chromium	38
Cobalt	44
coinage metals	48
Copper	48

D
Darmstadtium	6

F
Fluorine	100

G
Gold	60
Group I	10
Group II	20
Group III	64
Group IV	70
Group V	80
Group VI	90
Group VII	98
Group VIII	108

H
halogen elements	98
Helium	110
Hydrogen	8

I
Iodine	106
Iron	42

K
Krypton	116

L

lanthanides	118
Lead	78
Lithium	12

M

Magnesium	24
Manganese	40
Mercury	62
Molybdenum	52

N

Neon	112
Nickel	46
Nitrogen	82
nitrogen elements	80
noble gases	108

O

Oxygen	92
oxygen elements	90

P

Palladium	53
periodic table	6
Phosphorus	84
Platinum	58
Plutonium	122
Potassium	16

R

Radium	31
Radon	117
Rubidium	18

S

Selenium	96
Silicon	74
Silver	54
Sodium	14
Strontium	28
Sulphur	94

T

Tellurium	97
Tin	76
Titanium	34
transactinides	124
transition elements	32
Tungsten	56

U

Uranium	120

V

Vanadium	36

Z

Zinc	50

GLOSSARY

Alchemy Medieval attempts to convert base metals to Gold.

Alloy A mixture of metals.

Alpha particle A positively charged particle (a Helium nucleus) given off during some types of radioactive decay.

Atom The fundamental building block of matter.

Beta particle A negatively charged particle (an electron) given off during some types of radioactive decay.

Catalyst A substance that speeds up a chemical reaction.

Compound A substance created by the chemical bonding of elements.

Electron A sub-atomic particle with a negative charge.

Element A substance that cannot be broken down further by chemical reaction.

Gamma ray High-energy electromagnetic radiation given off by some nuclei.

Group A vertical column of elements on the periodic table. These elements often have closely related properties.

Ion A charged particle formed when an atom loses or gains electrons.

Ionization The process of producing ions.

Isotope Atoms of the same element that have the same number of protons and electrons but differing numbers of neutrons.

Neutron A sub-atomic particle with a neutral charge.

Nucleus The centre of an atom where protons and neutrons are found.

Oxide A compound of one element with Oxygen.

Particle accelerator A machine that can produce new elements by colliding charged particles at high speeds.

Period A horizontal row of elements on the periodic table.

Proton A sub-atomic particle with a positive charge.

Radioactivity Spontaneous disintegration of certain nuclei accompanied by the emission of alpha, beta or gamma radiation.

Salts Compounds formed when the Hydrogen ions in an acid are replaced by metal ions or other positive ions.